Thoughts In Motion

A Poetry Collection

Susana Martinez

BookLeaf Publishing

India | USA | UK

Made with ❤ on the BookLeaf Publishing Platform
www.bookleafpub.in
www.bookleafpub.com

Dedication

To anyone who thinks their writing is not good enough for the world to see, just do it. You'll be glad you did.

"If your dreams do not scare you, they are not big enough." - Ellen Johnson Sirleaf

Preface

This short poetry book contains collections of poems written throughout the years. Some old, some new, but all words that come from the heart. It's a mixture of my personal take on life's beauty, love, family, and uplifting thoughts. My hope is that anyone who reads these poems, can resonate or take something away from it. May you continue walking your path forward knowing that there is always something beautiful in life to love and appreciate.

Acknowledgements

To my husband Sonny, thank you for always believing in me.

I love you.

Us

Thoughtful and caring
Sweet and kind
All characteristics hard to find.
When we crossed paths,
We both knew
These traits were in me
As they were in you.
Let's continue this journey
Both you and I
As you show me your heart
And I give you mine.

Desert Skies

Pink fiery sky
I am mesmerized
Focus my eyes
On the colors above me
Cotton candy sky
Cool breeze passes by
I take this all in
It's astounding.

Blessings

My heart exploded
When your eyes met mine
My life's forever changed
Your little hand in mine
You're a blessing from above
God, I am so blessed
I'm grateful for this moment
I'm thankful for this day.

Home

Home is where the sun
Shines brightly on my face
Home is my small town
Where I spent most summer days
Home holds many memories
Many when I was young
I love to go back home
I'm proud where I come from.

Invincible

She thought she was invincible
Nothing could ever break her
Turned away from all the chaos
Even when it always chased her

Running got her nowhere
But to face the chaos alone
Still she felt invincible
Stronger than before

Where did this strength come from?
And was she really alone?
The truth is God was with her
But this she's always known

So she kept her head up high
With the path to the unknown.

How Beautiful It Is

6

Cotton candy skies
In this desert home of mine
How beautiful it is
His creation

Seasons change
Blessings given every day
How beautiful it is
His creation

I Choose Happiness

I choose happiness
What's the point of living in fear?
When I could find some good in each and every day
Today I opened my eyes
Today I could breathe
Today I have my loved ones
They're all I really need

I choose happiness
What's the point of living in anger?
Today I am at peace
Today I have let go
Today I will embrace those around me
They're the ones who love me most

I choose happiness
What's the point of being sad?
Today I am grateful
Today I heard laughter
Today I saw smiles
I choose happily ever afters

Younger Me

When I look into the mirror
I see the younger me
The girl who dreamed so big
Not knowing what would be

She dreamed of things so out of reach
Always tried to find a way
There was a drive deep inside
She knew she couldn't stay

She left her home, got on the road
Tears rolling down her face
The sunrise was her light
She wiped those tears away

The hardest move she had to make
Was leaving home behind
Younger me was chasing dreams
Not knowing what she'd find

Looking back to all the things
Younger me had faced
I'm so proud she never gave up
I'm so glad she gave herself grace.

Now I stare back at younger me
Feeling tears of joy
She reached her goals and so much more
All better than before.

Don't Give Up

Don't give up
Don't lose hope
Have some faith
The days seem long
But you'll find your happiness
Don't give up.

Tomorrow

Tomorrow isn't promised
So do it all today
Let go of what does not serve you
Say what you need to say
Tomorrow isn't promised
Hug the ones you love
Tell them how you feel
You can never say it enough.

Summer Night

It was one summer night
We talked for hours about life
This felt right
There was no fear
The start of something new
It all began here

Community

Community is togetherness

Community is support

Community needs one another

Community is love

Free Spirit

14

Free spirit travel far
See the world
Don't be afraid
Fly like a bird
Smile at others
Stay happy and kind
Be yourself
Have your own ideas
See what you find

Apa

Apa you are my hero
Since I was very young
I've seen all you've accomplished
You showed it can be done.

Apa you've watched me grow
Long talks and advice
You wanted to prepare me
Of the world I'd get to know

Apa you made my games
You showed up when it mattered
To see you in the crowd
Didn't take me long to scatter

Apa I watch you grow now
Once strong now a little fragile
You're still my hero though
There's nothing you can't handle

Apa I'm here for you
I'll always make you proud
Thank you for all your love
I've never gone without.

One Day

16

One day you'll understand
One day you'll get it right
One day you'll see why
One day you'll win the fight
One day you'll feel at peace
One day...

Nature

The beauty the wonder
The brightness of colors
The trees and the mountains
The smell of fresh air
The sound of a fire
The light from the moon
The beauty of nature
The adventure comes soon

Life

18

Life is beautiful
It's what you make of it
Make an impact
Make the very best of it.

Opinions

19

It's okay to disagree
As long as we're respectful
We can all think differently
Without being resentful

Growth

Growth takes time
Be proud of where you are
When you look back
You'll see how far you've come.

Mother

Mother mother
How was your day
Mine was so fun
I ran and I played

Mother mother
My heart is broken
What is this feeling
Why wasn't I chosen?

Mother mother
Today is moving day
I'll come back to visit
I'll call every day

Mother mother
I met the man of my dreams
He is the one
It feels meant to be

Mother mother
I'm having a boy!
I'm so excited
I'm overjoyed

Mother mother
I'm lucky to have you
You're my best friend
I love you my mother

Empty Road

For miles I'll drive
Talking to the moon
On this empty road
Till it gets me back to you.